What Is Liberalism?

A Guide for Progressives, Moderates, and Conservatives in America

by Anthony Signorelli

Copyright © 2018 Anthony Signorelli

All commercial rights reserved. No part of this work may be used or reproduced in any manner without written permission except in the case of brief quotations embodied in critical articles and reviews, with full attribution given to the author and publisher.

ISBN-13: 978-1724335135
ISBN-10: 1724335138

Published by Blue Harbor Press

559 Humboldt Avenue
Saint Paul, Minnesota 55107
651-340-2196

Print copies are available at Amazon.com.

About the Author

Anthony Signorelli is the author of several books on postcapitalism and political philosophy. He also blogs and publishes Intertwine, a regular email for deep hearts and vital minds.

To join the conversation and find out more about these books and Intertwine, please visit

http://anthonysignorelli.com/books

Table of Contents

Preface 1
Introduction 3

CHAPTER ONE 7
   Modern and Pre-Modern Consciousness 7
   The Religious Expression of Liberal Consciousness 11
   The Economic Expression of Liberal Consciousness 14
   The Political Expression of Liberal Consciousness 17

CHAPTER TWO 21
   How Did Liberal Principles Arise from Modern
   Consciousness? 21
   Private Property 23
   Rule of Law 28
   Sovereignty of the Individual 33

CHAPTER THREE 37
   Values in a Liberal Society 37
   The Progressive Modality 40
   The Moderate Modality 44
   The Conservative Modality 47
   Reclaiming the Words 51

CHAPTER FOUR 53
   True Conservatives Disenfranchised 53

CHAPTER FIVE 61
   American Liberal Principles 61
   Declaration of Independence 62
   The Constitution 65
   Bill of Rights 68

   Conclusion 71
   About the Author 75

Preface

It is May of 2018, and I am stunned at the current relevance of this essay, which was originally published twelve years ago. At the time, I was concerned that the corrosive discourse in American politics would lead us into extremism and away from our shared liberal principles. The primary culprit was the so-called liberal-conservative split which had marginalized true conservatives and given right wing extremism an air of legitimacy in the discussion.

With the rise of Trumpism, my fears are being realized. I don't publish this essay now as an "I told you so" response, but rather to remind people again of how this happened and what we need to understand about the basic principles of our liberal American democracy—that it requires true progressives, moderates, and conservatives to function, that the underlying principles of liberal democracy are far different than those of the right wing in this country today, and that these philosophies are reflected in the basic founding documents of the nation. Perhaps the most dangerous phenomenon we see today is the disenfranchisement of so many true conservatives. I documented their disenfranchisement in this essay, but it is also reflected in the number of true conservatives turning away from the Republican Party—members of congress, leading traditional conservatives, and increasing numbers of voters and party members. These defections illustrate the impact on the conservative voice in the country, but they are also giving space to right wing extremists to make their voices, policy positions, and priorities heard… and implemented. The damage being done is not simply to the policy structures one may disagree with Trump about; rather, it is the damage to the fabric of our political-social lives. We are legitimating extremism in America.

So, I am republishing this essay with minor edits for clarification, and no changes to the primary ideas and presentation of the material. Let it stand as a testimony that we have been in this process of breakdown in the body politic for a long time, and that it is getting worse. Xenophobia and hatred are being touted as acceptable; stupidity and thoughtlessness as normal; autocracy as merely a flavor of democracy. These ideas infect the brains and thought processes of more and more Americans. We must feed ourselves with truth and insight to preserve the principles of liberal democracy. I hope that this book is one of those that will feed your mind the thoughts and ideas you need.

--Anthony Signorelli, May 2018

Introduction

Contemporary American political discourse is destroying liberty—yours, mine, and that of all Americans. The notion of a divide between liberals and conservatives serves the political task of dividing people, confusing the argument, and obfuscating reality. Americans are susceptible to it because the words have been hijacked for the purpose of creating that confusion and turning us against each other. While Americans are focusing on demonizing each other as liberals or conservatives, other forces are staking a claim to legitimacy in our political debate. Right wing extremism masquerades as conservatism, "progressives" deny that they are liberal, and large groups of traditionalists argue for a return to some pre-modern state of purity which never existed. All the while, anti-modern, anti-liberty foundations are being laid, and movements are taking hold.

The method is confusion and obfuscation. Because we confuse the words liberal and conservative, we do not understand the arguments.

For example, our misunderstanding of the terms leads us to tolerate the hateful speech of a US Congressman who said we should send the "liberals" to Iraq to use as human shields for the troops. Understand what he said—take American citizens who he and his audience do not like and send them to certain death because he and his "conservative" friends dislike "liberals." The outrageousness of this statement by Rep. Jim Gibbons in the early 2000s is matched only by the acquiescent silence that followed from most of the American citizenry. We

Americans are losing our way in this discussion because we accept such language—even from our elected representatives—as "conservative" rants, whereas they are actually calculated political acts which undermine the very fabric of our political dialog. Americans accept these statements as appropriate "conservative" rhetoric. As I intend to demonstrate, it is neither appropriate nor conservative, and is aimed squarely at the disenfranchisement of all those who think differently from the congressman.

As I will demonstrate in the following pages, we live in a modern liberal society, and that is precisely what gives us our liberty. It is the foundation of American freedom. When we demonize "liberal" in our discourse, we are demonizing the very ideas that make America what it is. While some will say that's not what they mean, demonizing that word will always reverberate in the psyche to undermine liberal principles. Yet truly liberal ideas and principles—like private property, individual sovereignty, and rule of law—are precisely those that shook us out from under tyranny—kings, aristocracy, feudalism, and theocracy.

This is a very dangerous game. People who seek to undermine those very principles are supportive of, if not directly behind, the demonization of the word "liberal." Within our country, there are plutocrats who seek to control everything. There are theocrats who seek to turn America away from religious freedom and into a church-based state. There are even socialist-communists who seek state control, although their voices are fairly dim at this point it time. From outside our country, we battle ISIS-al Qaeda, an ideology that also explicitly seeks totalitarian religious control in the form of a so-called Islamic caliphate. We also remain locked in an ideological battle with Russia and China, North Korea and Iran, and the underlying issues are the same—these countries reject liberal principles of societal organization in favor of centralized control for political, economic, or religious purposes. We Americans rightly battle ISIS and these other states because they are anathema to what we believe in—western modernity and its liberal worldview. On the other hand, we rarely see the threat within our own world view and society, for it is buried deep in this fiction of a liberal-conservative battle. The fiction of the liberal-conservative split provides a hiding place, on both sides, for truly non-liberal, un-American ideas.

My purpose in this book is to re-establish the basis of three key words in our discourse—American, modern, and liberal. When we hear the word liberal demonized, we need to realize it is not just referring to the so-called "left" of the political spectrum. Rather, it echoes through history and affects our perception of liberal society. We need to understand that demonizing liberal is also indicting the very idea of modern liberal thought, and all the ways that it is different from pre-modern thought structures. Indeed, we need to understand that when liberal is being demonized, so is America, and that in fact, America's worst enemies all demonize liberal principles as they attack America itself. If we do not understand these realities, we are susceptible to passively accept in our own minds the demonizations being perpetrated by the media, plutocrats, and theocratic interests within our country. The moment we become passive to the foundation of our liberty, we begin to lose it. For all our problems and challenges, we Americans are still some of the most fortunate people on earth. There are still far more people trying to get into our country than there are trying to get out. But maintaining our good fortune requires vigilance, discipline of thought, and deep understanding.

CHAPTER ONE

Modern and Pre-Modern Consciousness

Any meaningful discussion of liberal political culture must begin with differentiating modern and pre-modern consciousness. To understand that difference, we have to go back to the origins of modernity itself, which most historians agree began with the Renaissance.

Pre-modern worldviews have been described by many theorists (Wilber, Habermas, etc.) as having archaic, magical, and mythic worldviews; that is, life was experienced largely as an undifferentiated whole. As organizing principles of society, politics, religion, and economics were essentially the same. In other words, leaders (politics) were appointed by gods (religion) who would determine if there was enough food (economics)—except that these different terms I have used—politics, religion and economics—would not be different. They would all point to the same thing, and in essence, be the same experience.

This nondifferentiation was based on a particular way of thinking and perceiving the world. Indeed, the essence of pre-modern consciousness—the feudal, Middle-Ages type—is domination by powerful people, gods, and archetypes; empire, honor, and glory; the early sense of self as separate from the tribe, yet not fully differentiated;

righteous order, rigid social hierarchy, and literal belief systems.[1] Material progress is won mostly by conquest.[2] Religious experience is mediated. All around you at all times and all places, life is experienced through the power of authorities *outside oneself*—as if you cannot know anything unless someone else tells you it is so. Honor, order, duty, obedience, allegiance—these were the psychic currencies of pre-modern consciousness, and they went hand-in-hand with a feudal church-state partnership and the economy of conquest. Although variation means that different aspects are stronger in different locations at different times, the general trend of pre-modern society and consciousness takes this non-differentiated form. This medieval, pre-modern consciousness dominated the Western world throughout the entire historical period we now call the Dark Ages and Medieval times.

In contrast, modern consciousness arose based on new perceptions and bases of thought. The man most often cited for ushering in this new consciousness is René Descartes' (1596-1650). Although he has been charged frequently with killing off the animated worldviews of peasants and primitives, Descartes' real enemy was the scholasticism of the dark ages[3]—in other words, the undifferentiated world. This worldview included the primitive animated worldview, but really focused on the feudal form of pre-modern consciousness. His famous dictum "I think, therefore I am" and his work asserting a mechanistic worldview are often criticized today as the

---

[1] Wilber, Ken. *A Thoery of Everything,* Shambala, 2000. pp. 9-10.
[2] Friedman, Benjamin. *The Moral Consequences of Economic Growth.* Alfred A. Knopf, New York, 2005.
[3] Aczel, Amin. *Descartes Secret Notebook,* Broadway Books, New York, 2005.

disaster that ushered in our hyper-rational world. In reality, Descartes was actually destroying scholasticism and pre-modern consciousness. He believed that individual experience is a better guide to reality. Such experience, together with the power of reason, became the bedrock upon which modern society was built. Through Descartes' new ideas (and with the help of many other thinkers over time) politics, economics, and religion began to differentiate. By differentiate, I mean that they became increasingly separated realms of human activity and societal organization. We will see how each of these realms was affected shortly.

Descartes' first book, *Discourse on Method,* was popular throughout Europe, even though it drew him many enemies. It was popular because it awoke consciousness, and in particular, an increased awareness of the self, and the individual's ability to know via his own experience. As people began to trust their own experience and empirical sensibility, the focal point of knowledge shifted away from the king, clergy or nobleman as arbiter of reality. The psychic currency of honor, order, duty, and allegiance crumbled. The mediating offices of king, clergy, and nobleman, each specific to their own realm of politics, religion, and economics, became disenfranchised against the new consciousness. Instead, people trusted themselves, their own senses, their own experience. Mind you, this did not all happen in a few days, or months, or even years. The change and ultimate disenfranchisement of these powers took centuries, but their roots maybe found in Descartes.

The pioneers of modernity had a very hard time of it with these new ideas and the inherent differentiations. Galileo went to prison for his science, Descartes went on the run for his ideas, and even da Vinci was forced to carry out his scientific work in secret, especially his anatomical dissections.[4] The battles would go on for centuries, including the 18th Century's Enlightenment and the 20th Century's battle over evolution which continues to this day. Yet, there was no way to develop backwards. The erosion of the old, pre-modern consciousness of honor-order-duty-allegiance had begun, and a new, modern consciousness based on direct individual experience, rational thought, and free economic exchange began to emerge.

Under pre-modern consciousness religion, economics, and politics are merged into one confusing mass in order for the system to function. Political power is bestowed by god, economic power by political or religious decree and the whole thing is based on principles of honor, order, duty, and allegiance. Society is organized by positions into which one is born. However, when the baseline consciousness of western society changed, and people began to see, think, perceive, and experience for themselves, those thoughts and perceptions could only pull apart the undifferentiated mass that appeared before them. Hence, the modern differentiations came into being. Modern consciousness separated I, we, and it; it differentiaed art, morals, and science; it pulled apart the key social structures of religion, economics, and politics, In doing so, it developed and discovered the basic principles of modern liberal society.

For many people, this differentiation was experienced as a crumbling of their world, and so it encountered fierce resistance. On one hand, the entrenched powers of the

---

[4] Capra, Fritjof. *The Science of Leonardo: Inside the Mind of the Great Genius of the Renaissance*. Doubleday, New York, 2007.

church and the state fought these ideas with suppression movements like the Inquisitions. On the other, common people were confused at the loss of meaning and the accompanying anxiety. Hence, the differentiation and all that it offered was set to conflict with the pre-modern view. The bigger the claims made by modern consciousness, the bigger the backlashes, reactions, and responses. Most of these reactions sought not to correct and preserve the modern consciousness, but rather to put the clock back and undo the modern insights and differentiations altogether. Indeed, this is the very battle we find ourselves in today.

The Religious Expression of Liberal Consciousness

During the Middle Ages, western society was dominated for about 1,000 years by the feudal-church partnership.[5] The religious component of this partnership was essentially Christian, and the Christian religious experience was mediated by the Roman Catholic Church or the Eastern Orthodox Church and their off-shoots. Christians experienced God through their clergy and clergy-mediated sacraments: mass, penance, marriage, and baptism. They prayed and worshipped by adhering to the structure and rules established by the church, absolved sins in confession, and received blessings through participation in communion. The church was always

---

[5] Lindsay, Thomas M. *A History of the Reformation.* New York, Charles Scribner's Sons, 1916.

positioned *between* the people and their God so that the people got to God through the clergy. This structure also guaranteed the church's sole access to knowledge (religion), its position of power within the society (politics), and its economic ability to amass wealth (economics). Hence, the church was deeply invested in the pre-modern, undifferentiated world.

The Reformation was a direct challenge to this mediated experience and the authority structure it maintained. Martin Luther posited the view that individuals could have a direct *relationship* with God, and therefore God could be *experienced* directly. Notice the similarity to Descartes' focus on individual experience? You didn't need a priest. You didn't need a church. Rather, one could know God through one-to-one prayer and direct study of the Bible. Gutenberg's printing press produced the Bible in the common languages of the people, so they could read and contemplate it themselves. Luther, together with the new bibles and the spread of literacy, enabled Protestantism to thrive. The church's power eroded as it became increasingly disenfranchised, although its endurance even to this day is testimony to the power it wielded.

In Christianity, this protestant idea and its notion of directly experiencing God developed in two directions. The first went beyond the questions of authority and knowledge, and encouraged a follower to model one's individual life on Jesus. Rather than following the rules of a mysterious and often manipulative clergy, worshippers modeled their lives on the morality of Jesus himself, who said, "Love your enemy," and "What you do to the weakest among you, you do unto me." Jesus rebelled against the rule-making power structure of the Pharisees, and he preached diversity, tolerance and love. "Let you who has not sinned cast the first stone." Christ provided an image to which one should aspire. Based as it was on direct, individual experience, this was a *liberal* theology. A radical new unfolding of religious consciousness was at hand.

The second direction, however, tried to retain the old power relationships of the feudal-church structure based on pre-modern consciousness. John Calvin led a major part of the Protestant movement to turn the "authority figure" of the feudal-church structure away from the church—with its priests, rituals and hierarchical institutions—and place the authority in the Holy Bible alone. The Bible came to be viewed as the true Word of God. Because the Word of God is supposedly clear, the individual had little discretion in how he experienced God. God's Word, the direct experience of him, the moral code and how to behave are all stated obviously in the literal words of the Bible. The Bible amounts to God's commands to his followers. Known then as Calvinism, revivalism, and Puritanism, this perspective has become our modern day fundamentalism. It is a way to destroy liberal theology using its own tools, as much as possible. The liberal notion, "Decide for yourself," was replaced by the Puritan command, "Read it for yourself." The freedom of the new modern liberal consciousness was sacrificed to a new, impersonal authority, the comfort of "knowing" the truth, and a clear delineation of morality. The only real difference was that it didn't rely on a priest intermediary, but it left the control and the struggle with morality outside oneself; thereby comfortably pre-modern. Liberty, with its attendant ambiguity and responsibilities, gave way to control by the Word, with its moral clarity and rigidity. Religious power accrued to those who quoted the Bible with the most authority, spoke the most loudly, and translated and printed the most Bibles. Hence, the essential honor-order-duty structure of pre-modern consciousness remained unchanged—except that instead of dutifully obeying one's lord or baron or priest, one simply obeyed the book. In this second direction, literalism usurped modern liberal thought.

The Economic Expression of Liberal Consciousness

Just as religious experience and perspective underwent a radical shift at the birth of modernity, so did the economic system. Until then, economic well-being was based primarily on the honor-order-duty system of feudalism and aristocracy. Land, the basis of all wealth, was granted by nobility. Many people had no land, and so practiced crafts, but only if they had access to guilds (usually determined by birth) or patrons. Still others tried to enter the clergy. Because of the total dependence of all levels on these relationships, exploitation was easy and widespread.

Despite the many attempts to conjoin religion and economics (e.g., Calvinism, Puritanism's "elect," and today's gospel of success), economics was differentiating itself from church (religion) and government (politics). As Protestantism grew, and as the roots of democratic rule formed, free enterprise developed as a differentiated economic system. Free enterprise—an idea that could not even be conceived under pre-modern consciousness—built its identity on individual experience, reason, and observation as the source of knowledge, just as the religion and politics differentiated similarly.

The term "private enterprise" expresses these principles in the area of human economic behavior. Economics based on modern consciousness requires that free people allocate risk and reward according to merit and performance rather than privilege and position. The only alternatives to modern economics are pre-modern systems such as aristocracy or feudalism which do not differentiate, and nationalist systems like communism, fascism, and certain incarnations of socialism, which quickly collapse into cronyism, or economics by position.

When we consider free enterprise, we should not confuse the *system* of capitalism with liberal economic *philosophy* of free enterprise. The liberal philosophy of free enterprise calls for resources and capital to be allocated according to the development of wealth as individuals and groups of individuals see fit. Individuals determine what works for them. Such an economics not only optimizes the fiscal independence of the individual—a core liberal value—but also protects political freedom (and differentiation) by enabling individuals to legally obtain the tools essential to political expression, religious expression, and intellectual freedom. This freedom to decide the deployment of capital is deeply connected to the political freedom of expression because without economic freedom, one cannot have access to printing presses, Internet servers, the electricity which runs them, or the paper on which to print political messages and ideas. The freedom to deploy capital also places economic control in the hands of the people who carry the economic consciousness.

The reason we need to separate the *system* of capitalism from the liberal economic *philosophy* of free enterprise is that economics, just like religion, split in two directions. The truly liberal direction we just described. Just as religion found a way to maintain pre-modern consciousness through literalism and fundamentalism, economics found a way to do it through the industrial revolution and corporate power. The economic sphere quickly created trusts, corporations, and other structures to defend old wealth against the new freedom, and also to become the method of investing and creating new wealth. But the corporate became the bureaucratic, and so functionally was no different than the old wealth by position economy. "Network" and "access" replaced the old reliance on whose son you were, but as so many people discovered for so many centuries, in this system, it still matters whose son you are because that's what gets you in the doors that provide network and access.

Thus the corporate structure became a bastion of pre-modern thought processes, with only the slightest coating of liberty shaken into it. Hierarchically, they have a king at the top, and each little slice of the hierarchy has a "boss." Sometimes, the bosses have to work together, sometimes not. But the "subordinate" must always do what he is told, or he will be "fired"—calling to mind that gruesome practice of burning insubordinates, otherwise known as heretics, at the stake. A worker's life is lived in similar relationship to the boss as the life of peasants to the hobbles of the aristocracy and feudalism.

Hence, with both religion and economics, the modern idea and the liberal program arise, but they are immediately usurped by a structure made possible by modernity. This structure is clearly not liberal because its habits of thought, perception, and relationship all reflect pre-modern perspectives. The great duality of our culture is not between science and religion, as so many have mistakenly argued. Rather, the great duality of contemporary life is between these two manifestations of modernity—the liberal one based on modern thought, and the nonliberal approach based on pre-modern consciousness.

The Political Expression of Liberal Consciousness

Politics underwent perhaps the most wrenching changes as modernity dawned. Politics refers to the power structures and governing structures of the society. The pre-modern structures were primarily based on a sense of nobility, a strong man, or position. Remember, it was honor, order, duty, and allegiance. Those are primarily political terms in a pre-modern context, for position and power were *conferred*, not earned. Even the king or emperor was thought to be in their position by being *conferred* to it by God himself.

As modernity blossomed, the underlying change toward trusting individual experience led to the enfranchisement of individuals. Enfranchised individuals began to see that what they needed was not the position conferred by a failing emperor, but the rights that they should have by virtue of their very existence. This awareness was reflected when the English barons asserted the Magna Carta against King John of England in the 13th century. That document was the first assertion of an emerging idea of private property, but also the first assertion of individual rights. Their assertion presaged all that was to come in the development of liberal political institutions.

The political realm was not free from its own set of usurpers either. Just as modernity gave religion and economics two different directions of development, so it did in politics. As the sense of individual political rights changed and grew, people began to think of themselves as citizens, with a power center of rights and ability to take action rooted in their very being, as opposed to owing all their power and position to someone who conferred it. Hence, the notion of the sovereign individual became the basis of democratic revolutions—and it still is. Because of the threat to stability, the immediate response was to maintain monarchies in countries that had them, chiefdoms where they have those, and emperors where they had those. Known as "constitutional monarchies," this strange duality arose in many places in Europe as a way of preserving the old pre-modern structures, while tipping a hat to the newly sovereign individual.

As the monarchies have largely become ceremonial reminders of an old heritage, they have been slowly replaced by jolts of state control. The most poignant example is the Russian Revolution that brought communism to power. Not long afterward, the Twentieth centuries horrors of fascism and national socialism (Nazism) also developed. These were also thoroughly modern in their scope, technical ability, and organizational structure, yet they were operated n thoroughly pre-modern thought structures. Hannah Arendt criticized the German people for their passivity under Nazism without ever identifying that Nazism could only get a foothold where pre-modern consciousness was widespread. Both the structure of its ranks, as well as the power wielded in society and through the entire industrial complex of Germany required this pre-modern consciousness to serve that kind of state interest. Honor, order, duty, allegiance. They make the work of the tyrant so much simpler.

The differentiation of religion, politics, and economics uniquely distinguishes modernity from all pre-modern organizing principles of social organization. These two forms of consciousness continue to battle for dominance in our contemporary world, with fundamentalism being the primary force against modern consciousness. In this way, there is more similarity between the American Christian fundamentalists and the Islamic fundamentalists of ISIS an al Qaeda than most people realize. American Christian fundamentalists want to turn the USA into a Christian nation that dissolves the modern differentiation of church and state. The Islamic fundamentalists decry what they call "the great schism" of western thought, and seek to create their own Islamic caliphate—a religiously based state that would dissolve the differentiation. These fundamentalists have a common enemy based on a shared mode of consciousness. The ultimate goal—the reversal of modern consciousness is the same—even if the admissible tactics for achieving those goals appear to be drastically different.

CHAPTER TWO

How Did Liberal Principles Arise from Modern Consciousness?

People who see the world through the prism of the liberal-conservative split usually think of anything *liberal* as a hotbed of radicalism or debauchery. It's the old drugs, sex, and rock-n-roll stereotype—an image created for the purpose of creating that split. If you think that way, take a breath and consider these outlandish *liberal* principles: Private property, Rule of Law, individual sovereignty. To people who believe in the liberal-conservative split, these ideas would be labeled *conservative*, but actually, they are radically *liberal* ideas.

The principles of private property, rule of law, and individual sovereignty disenfranchised the powers of the time. Entire revolutions were fought to affect the change embodied in these principles. Shall we have private property or an aristocracy? Who will make the laws—an arrogant king asserting his will or representatives of the people? To whom must we each bow? To a king on a throne, or to the "sovereign king" seeking to be free within each of us? These principles hung together to wrench freedom from the grips of feudal aristocracy, and that aristocracy knew it. Blood was spilt and wars were fought because the old structures could not survive in a society built on these new principles.

Modern consciousness started somewhere around 1500. In the 1700s, leading European Enlightenment thinkers such as Locke, Smith, Hume, Voltaire and Rousseau developed that consciousness into these and other principles, while famous American leaders like Thomas Jefferson and James Madison enshrined them into constitutional government. Today, many of them are eroding through mockery, ignorance, and purposeful destruction, much of which begins with the fiction of the so-called liberal-conservative split. Our minds are muddied when we demonize the word liberal, and therefore can't see the liberal nature of these ideas, or when we demonize the word conservative, and can't recognize the foundation of our country. To get out of this, we have to better understand these three basic principles, among the many others on which our freedom and liberty are based.

Before we investigate these principles, one important distinction must be made: Principles are not values. Principles are objective and enduring; they exist outside one's personal judgment. Principles change slowly over centuries or millennia. In contrast, values are individualized and subjective, based on the individual's assessment at any given time, and reflect the individual's imperfect and changing knowledge and perspective. Our values change as we grow. This change is natural and necessary, but it makes values a frivolous foundation for cultural development. You may or may not value private property, but it remains a principle of modern society.

You may or may not value Rule of Law, but it endures as a modern principle of the liberal worldview.

I can already hear the howling: "I believe in x-y-z so strongly it is the most important principle of my life!" Get over yourself. A strongly held value is an important, strongly held value. It is not a principle. Values build people, principles form cultures.

Private Property

The principle of private property is one of the central pillars of liberal society, the mechanism by which enormous power is wrested from a noble aristocracy and placed in the hands of the people. Property is to be owned by people with the ability to leverage it—sell, buy, mortgage, and so on. Hence, private property transfers wealth and power to the people, and provides the means for the creation of wealth which underlies the entire economic system. It establishes the capital base of the individual family, and fuels entrepreneurship, financial security and the economic creativity of society.

Various concepts of property date very far back in European history, but private property—as an alternative to the feudal system of property—was embraced more fundamentally as the Renaissance emerged, and the question was debated by philosophers—Thomas Hobbes, James Harrington (later celebrated by John Adams) John Locke, William Blackstone, and David Hume. In the 1600s, Harrington clearly identified private property as an instrument which could be used to disempower tyranny. John Locke investigated the question of when an apple on a tree becomes private property. These were serious ideas deserving serious thought because of their consequences.

At the outset, private property radically challenged an arbitrary land tenure system previously dependent on the whims of the king and the nobility. If an individual holding tenure of land under the old system committed even a slight offense against the king, and the king then felt compelled a year or two later to reward someone else, and looked for land to grant, he might recall the offense. The land could then be taken away from the "less honorable" man and bestowed on the more "worthy" man. The result was arbitrary control of the land based on the whims of kings, lords, barons, and dukes.

The concepts of title and private ownership remove the arbitrary power of this aristocracy to determine land ownership, and profoundly empower private landowners; changes in land tenure occur by way of transactions between people rather than custom or royal decree. The wealth represented by the land is freed as a source of investment capital, and landowners are enabled to act on their own behalf. Today, we accept this situation as a basic assumption. We assume, for example, that most people have the potential own homes and land, but it was not always that way, and still is not in many parts of the world. Looking at much of the Third World one can see the results of economies built without private property principles.

Hernando de Soto, President of the Institute for Liberty and Democracy in Peru, and author of *The Mystery of Capital*,[7] documents the lack of private property structures in Third World urban areas as a major factor contributing

---

[7] De Soto, Hernando. *The Mystery of Capital*. Basic Books, New York, 2002.

to the creation of a permanent underclass in the shantytowns of Mexico City, Lima, Rio de Janeiro, Bombay, and other areas around the world. Millions of people in these cities essentially live as squatters who own nothing. In every case, the lack of a functioning private property system contributes to the squalid poverty of these cities. The formal systems of the national governments are so unwieldy, complicated, bureaucratic, and inaccessible as to render them irrelevant to the majority of the people, who cannot claim ownership of the land on which they live, cannot transfer control of it, and therefore cannot borrow against it or leverage it.

De Soto's analysis shows that the lack of workable private property systems in such places has effectively locked up trillions of dollars in wealth. This frozen capital depresses the creative energy of the people and gives rise to whole new societal structures, most of them informal. The shantytowns develop their own unofficial enforcement mechanisms, their own informal police, their own illegal markets and tariff systems and other economic and political structures to establish some sense of ownership, order, and stability. Gangs, neighborhood bosses and other power centers emerge in the midst of the official power vacuum, thereby re-creating a kind of old world feudalism.[8]

---

[8] When this happened in America, we called it the "Wild West." One aspect of the American genius is that every time the population expanded into new areas, private property became the guiding principle establishing tenure on the land. The homestead programs, common law and squatter's rights were all part of the infrastructure of private property ownership. There was a very dark side to this: the land kept being taken from the Native Americans by the U.S. Government, primarily by war. Conquest, the dominant pre-modern tool for acquiring wealth, still functioned at the edge of the modern liberal democracy of America, and it was thoroughly

De Soto's analysis helps us to see the critical importance of private property in the creation and maintenance of a liberal economic system. In the past, the threat to private property principle was government; today, it is the corporation.

The increasing domination of the economy by corporate enterprise is a clear threat to the principle of private property. As a principle, private property puts the property in the control and ownership of the people, and ensures that such ownership changes and rotates as people and families change. Corporations are not people—they don't die, they can't go to prison, they don't vote, they do not have families. Corporations are institutions, similar to churches and governments. They are impersonal, bureaucratic, and controlled by people in positions of power—that is, by people who hold office. Corporate property essentially establishes "fiefdoms," where land is removed from citizen control and handed over to an "aristocratic" executive class who exercises arbitrary power over it. In most cases, the land never reverts to individual ownership, but is held in perpetuity by one corporation or another.

In other words, citizens are disenfranchised from the land, and the political power unleashed by the whole idea of private property is being usurped. Under the language of "private property", increasing amounts of land in all countries is moving into the hands of corporate

---

exploited. Once land was under the control of the U.S. government, however, it was systematically put into the hands of the people to be held as private property within the society. Hence, within the society, private property resulted in an enormous freeing of capital that has fueled the American economy.

institutions. Yet, corporations are not private entities—they are quasi-government organizations. Property owned by them is just as distant to the average citizen as property owned by the government, or the king, and the more property they control in aggregate, the deeper the erosion of private property in reality, and with it, the erosion of liberty, especially economic and political liberty.

While De Soto does not clearly address corporate ownership in the Third World, corporate ownership remains the primary tool for disenfranchising the people from their land and ensuring permanent subjugation of the population—both in the Third World *and* in modern liberal economies. The good land is taken from the indigenous people and descendants of immigrant farmers, often by force. The formal property system supports this theft by making it virtually impossible for the lower classes to assert any property rights. Denied ownership of the land, the people become only a labor pool while corporate or government interests exploit the land. In modern liberal economies such as the United States, corporate ownership has the same effect against indigenous people where they still have the land, and against every day citizens as well. Corporations claim rights, operate on a non-human scale, take land out of circulation, dig underneath privately controlled land and even clear cut and strip mine land owned by citizens with the backing of the government in the exercise of "mineral rights" and the like. It's as if all people, indigenous or not, are in the way. Resistance is derisively called "NIMBY"—Not In My Back Yard—by the powers that be. Or, to paraphrase one commentator from the 1990s, "We're all indigenous now."[9]

When corporate and government interests come together this way, modern consciousness is collapsing behind it. We are losing the differentiation of politics (government) and economics (corporations) in a profoundly anti-liberal, anti-modern shift, and a basic liberal principle, private property, is being made into a mockery. Since the economic basis of a modern liberal society is private property, we are all well-served to recognize threats to that principle.

Rule of Law

The Rule of Law was succinctly articulated by Immanuel Kant: "Man is free if he needs to obey no person but solely the laws." The Rule of Law frees citizens from the arbitrary or discretionary rule of individuals—kings, tyrants, communist planners, and despots—by establishing rules that create a stable, predictable environment within which people can act. It makes the actions of other people and the state reasonably predictable so that economic, political, religious, and social actions can be undertaken without fear of capricious exercise of authority to thwart one's efforts. The Rule of Law is not merely the bestowal of "legality" on decisions or actions; it is a deeper principle whose objectivity and uniformity is its central feature. As Kant says, that feature is the foundation of freedom.

---

[9] Jackson, Wes, *Becoming Native to this Place,* University Press of Kentucky, 1994

More recently, Nobel Laureate Friedrich A. Hayek, in his 1944 classic *The Road to Serfdom* wrote:

> Nothing distinguishes more clearly conditions in a free country from those in a country under arbitrary government than the observance in the former of the great principles known as the Rule of Law. Stripped of all technicalities, this means that government in all its actions is bound by rules fixed and announced beforehand—rules which make it possible to foresee with fair certainty how the authority will use its coercive powers in given circumstances and to plan one's individual affairs on the basis of this knowledge.[10]

Hayek echoes Kant—when the action of the state is pre-determined by law, citizens are enabled to plan their individual conduct with a reasonable ability to predict state action in regard to that conduct. But Hayek also further defines it. The Rule of Law is a complex concept which has four primary features. It is:

☐ **Nondiscretionary**: Rule of Law is objective, not subjective. It eliminates arbitrary or discretionary decisions.

☐ **Announced beforehand**: Rule of Law enables citizens to predict the manner in which the state will and will not act with regard to the citizen's affairs.

☐ **Uniformly applied**: Law applies to everyone; no person is above the law. Rule of Law has general applicability; it is not specific, nor exceptional.

☐ **Uniformly enforced**: Law is enforced evenly and equally on all citizens.

---

[10] Hayek, *op. cit.*, p. 80.

These four functions remove individual judgment or discretion in the wielding of the state's power. Authority is vested in the law itself, rather than in the judgment or discretion of a single person. Such law is objectively made, stated in public, easily knowable by the citizenry, and dependably enforced. As a result, individuals know what actions will get them into trouble with the state and what behavior is required in order to stay out of trouble. With this knowledge, the individual can act and make commitments with the confidence that economic, political, and religious competitors are not receiving unfair advantages.

In societies that are not under the Rule of Law, decisions of the state are discretionary and arbitrary. The state acts when an individual in authority *decides* to act, not when permitted or necessitated by the law. No person is free in such a state. No person can predict what is legal or illegal, allowable or unallowable, because those decisions are left up to the discretion of an individual. In pre-modern times, these powers were vested in a king or a feudal lord. In modern times, they are often vested in the authorities of state-run economies like the former Soviet Union, death squads or militaries run amok, or in the corruption of public institutions for private gain: especially through bribery, blackmail, and paying "fees" to get things done. These problems are commonly seen in those countries where there is little tradition of Rule of Law.[11]

---

[11] It must be noted that this principle must also apply at the community level. In the second half of 2014 and early 2015, many Americans became aware of the uneven application of this principle right here in communities of our own country. The rise of Black Lives Matter has been one expression of this realization. Too many of these principles have not been evenly

A critical distinction must be made between Rule of Law and "legality." Just because an action is "legal" does not mean it is in conformity with the Rule of Law. To the extent that a constitutional body creates a law that confers discretionary rule or power to an individual or governmental position, it is not conforming to the Rule of Law. Laws that confer such power are the basis of the "legal" legitimacy claims of despots and dictators—the dictator convinces or forces a legislative body to confer enormous discretionary power on him, or the dictator declares a crisis that enables him to take such power. In most cases, such moves are, strictly speaking, "legal" but in no way conform to the Rule of Law. Rather, the vesting of this subjective, discretionary authority in an individual creates inherent arbitrariness in the law. As the arbitrary potential increases, the liberty of the citizens decreases because there is no way to reasonably predict the actions of the state. In other words, while a legislative act may be "legal" or "lawful" in conferring arbitrary or discretionary power on a government official, such an act is not consistent with Rule of Law.

The rhetoric of the 2000-2008 Bush administration defended a broad range of actions as "lawful." American citizens ought to be wary. While it is possible that the government's treatment of detained prisoners and its program of spying on Americans are "lawful," they are clearly not consistent with the Rule of Law. In both cases, laws and findings have created a legal framework to justify the legal case for what they are doing, but the

---

applied, with the unevenness often misapplied on racial lines. The oppression experienced in many of our communities of color are places where this and the other great principles are not appropriately applied.

effect is to put discretionary power for these programs in the hands of the President. He alone decides if they are being properly administered. He alone decides if someone is an "unlawful combatant" and therefore subject to detainment at Guantanamo without any recourse to justice or legal representation. The President has argued it is legal, and he has argued the merits of the need. Reasonable people can disagree about the legality and the merits, but there is no question that the President's continued accumulation of discretionary power is counter to the fundamental principle of liberty known as the Rule of Law.[12]

Arbitrary enforcement can also undermine the Rule of Law. Enforcement of the law is the responsibility of the executive branch. Lack of uniform enforcement necessarily increases the arbitrariness and preferential aspect of the law. For example, when former Vice President Cheney was alleged to have intervened to stop enforcement of environmental regulations against mining companies, it was discretionary law enforcement. When government is so under-funded that it cannot achieve uniform enforcement, the result is arbitrary enforcement. In these cases, the dependability of enforcement is not based on objective criteria, but on one's relationship with certain individuals in the administration, the behavior of the state is no longer predictable, and liberty is diminished.

---

[12] While George W. Bush declared and consolidated this power, Barack Obama has done nothing to dismantle it, and in fact seems to have exercised it even further, as exposed by Edward Snowden's release of information related to the NSA.

Sovereignty of the Individual

Before liberal government came along, a nation's inhabitants were its "subjects." Webster's Third International Dictionary defines subject as: "one that is placed under the authority, dominion, control, or influence of someone or something." Ordinary people were subjected to the whims and concerns of an aristocracy, the king, their lord, their duke, their count, so one ca see why the pre-modern ethic of honor-order-duty-allegiance was so important; without it, the fundamental building block of societal organization could not stand. The entire infrastructure of the aristocracy was built on the hierarchy of subjects and that pre-modern consciousness.

Based on pre-modern consciousness, the West organized society according to "houses" and honor; what in other parts of the world even today, we would call clans. These forms of organization did not respect the individual being, except as a member of a house or family. If one man killed another, revenge might be taken out on the killer's brother, not the killer himself, and this was seen as just retribution. In essence, the killer's brother who died in retribution had no sovereignty or individuality at all—his only meaning being as a member of that particular clan. In other words, he was a token of honor to the clan, but the individual man had no sovereignty at all.[13]

Modern Americans are usually abhorred by these kinds of "honor killings" or "acts of honor revenge" because we

---

[13] Weiner, Mark S. *The Rule of the Clan,* Farrar, Strauss, & Giroux, New York, 2013.

think of ourselves as citizens. Everyone is a citizen. Rich and poor. Labor and owners. Urban and rural. We take this idea for granted, forgetting that it was not always the case, and usually unaware of the revolutionary aspect of the word. "Citizen" reflects the autonomy of the individual and a sense of mutual responsibility. In its simplest definition, the word refers to a member of a state. But the larger meaning conveys a sense of *reciprocity* between the individual and his or her government. Citizens are not subjected to anyone, but rather enter into a relationship with government, a relationship defined by mutual obligations of allegiance and protection, and a relationship entered into by *choice*. Citizens make the choice to be in government because the mutual defense is better achieved collectively than individually. In a liberal world individuals are full citizens; they are no longer mere subjects in a world of aristocrats.

This reality is why Descartes' vision of individual experience, the ensuing modern movement, and the Enlightenment a couple hundred years later, were viewed as so subversive and destabilizing to the existing power structures in church and state. In fact, they *were* destabilizing. From individual experience, it is a short leap to individual sovereignty, and no system of power based on denying individual sovereignty can survive when a general population believes in its own sovereignty more than it does the God-ordained power claimed by its clergy and kings. Not only were these issues central to the American Revolution, but they were also the underlying ideas leading to the French Revolution ten years later.

When individuals are sovereign beings in their own right, the lords and kings of aristocratic states no longer have the right to exert power over their supposed subjects because those subjects are *sovereign* beings in and of themselves. They owe no honor or allegiance to anyone. Sovereign means to have power, authority, independence, rightful status, or prerogative. Hence, the sovereign individual is to have that power or authority over himself or herself. Individual sovereignty is the source of our actual liberty. When the United States was formed by "The People," those very words expressed our sovereignty. We chose to come together to declare independence from Great Britain, and to create the government we would choose for ourselves.

Private property, Rule of Law, and individual sovereignty are three of the oldest liberal principles. These ideas are normally associated with conservative ideas, yet there they are at the very center of a liberal worldview. Far from the popular caricatures of liberalism, these and other principles form the foundation of the liberal philosophy that underlies our society and each has played a crucial role in the establishment of America and our basic principles. Virtually all of the rights we enjoy today owe their genesis to the philosophical exploration of these principles, which unfolded over centuries. Knowing that, we can now turn to that unique incarnation of liberal principles—America.

But before looking at how these principles manifested in a uniquely American way, we need to differentiate these *principles* from the values that define most of our contemporary political dialog. We turn to that task in the next chapter.

CHAPTER THREE

Values in a Liberal Society

As liberal *principles* provide an enduring foundation to liberal society, individual affiliation to those principles is mediated by *values*—the ever pliable, often changing viewpoint from which people live their actual lives. The principles underlying society are not usually in the forefront of thought and discussion because they are the assumptions on which it stands. They are "reality," and therefore not up for questioning and discussion. As a result, we pay these principles little attention unless they come under threat from forces either within or without our national borders.

Values, on the other hand, are the center point of most of our discussions and debates. For a very long time, the values conversation has been understood in binary terms—left vs. right, Democrats vs. Republicans, and in what we can now recognize as an inaccurate use of the term, liberal vs. conservative. Rather than viewing the wings of American politics as hostile to one another, I propose a re-imagining of the body politic that stands on the very foundation of liberal principles we have been discussing. This reimagining requires two changes in perspective.

The first change is to identify the three "modalities" of American political discourse, which we will name conservative, moderate, and progressive. Each modality constitutes a general viewpoint by raising certain values to the forefront of the perspective. We will investigate each of these shortly.

Second, we need to acknowledge that the threat to liberal principles does not come from one of the other modalities. Conservatives are not a threat to progressives, and moderates are not a threat to conservatives. What is a threat is the extreme *illegitimate, dissociated* position each modality can fall into as a system of ideas and thought. By *illegitimate*, I mean a position that has no contribution to make to the development or strengthening of liberal principles since the position itself opposes those very principles. By *dissociated*, I mean a position in which the values and ideas within the modality disconnect from the liberal principles and seek to elevate and dominate, denying any legitimacy to the other modalities, and which pretend its positions are not mere values, but actual principles in and of themselves. As we will see, these dissociated positions can occur in all three modalities. The problem is the illegitimate dissociation, not the values.

No doubt some will complain that the charge of illegitimacy is too harsh. It is not. While the three modalities—conservative, moderate, and progressive—are largely solid and accepted standpoints within liberal culture, each carries the potential for an extreme version which attacks and erodes liberal principles and liberal society. But let me issue a challenge—if one is going to attack liberal principles and society, one must posit a replacement. Conservative, moderate, and progressive modalities are creations of liberal principle. Each represents an alternative view among others, but it is built on liberal principles. While the modalities are legitimate, the alternatives to liberal democracy, such as communism, theocracy and fascism, are not legitimate. Despotism and cronyism are not legitimate alternatives, nor is aristocracy. Right wing extremism, which is an illegitimate dissociated conservatism, leads to many of those alternatives, such as fascism, theocracy, and plutocracy. Left-wing extremism, which is illegitimate dissociated progressivism, leads to alternatives like socialism and communism. All these alternative forms of political organization were, and should be, rejected in favor of liberal principles and organization. Such alternatives are appropriately described as illegitimate in a liberal world.

In order for these three styles of democracy to thrive again, Americans need to recognize the so-called "liberal-conservative split" as a false dialogue. This view creates a false enemy—the liberal—so that non-liberals may promulgate ideas like the unitary executive, the "values voter," and the ownership society. Acceptance of the so-called liberal-conservative split enables the right-wing to steal the legitimate name "conservative" and put it on an illegitimate, radical right-wing agenda, thereby making that agenda appear legitimate, palatable, reasonable, and mainstream. But it isn't reasonable, nor mainstream, nor for that matter *conservative*. Instead, the rhetoric drives ideological wedges based on the dissociated bifurcation of the political landscape, and the nuanced positions of real people get swept into one side or the other. This reality serves only those who demonize liberal society as much as they demonize the individuals they call liberal.

In reality, progressive, moderate, and conservative modalities all belong to the same spectrum of modern *liberal* thought. They each have legitimate viewpoints of politics, religion, and economics; each has an important contribution to make. And yet, each can easily slip into dissociated illegitimacy, where it claims it has the only answer and the others cannot contribute anything. At that point, the dialogue slips from debate, discussion and discovery, into advocacy by way of the loudest voice and the most money. To understand this, let's look at each modality in detail.

The Progressive Modality

The progressive modality draws its core energy from the human capacity to hope. Hope implies improvement in the future and provides the momentum for forward movement, for progress and the expression of the human creative drive. Hope inspires us to act, and serves as the creative energy of entrepreneurship, art, and social and political activism. Hope, or the promise of progress, is the torchlight guiding the commitment of new immigrants to work hard for a better future; it spurs small business people to risk everything in search of a better eventuality for their lives; it inspires service to the poor, work to alleviate poverty, and even the work of missionaries. Progress flows as a political energy based on the notion: *We can change this. We can do better.* In fact, the progressive questions repeat themselves over and over again: *What are we doing wrong? How can we do better? How can we be more fair? How can we release more of the spontaneous energy of liberty among more of our people? What is unjust and how do we fix it?*

Progressive energy is the source that builds things, and the driving force behind addressing perceived wrongs. Progressivism gave us the Hoover Dam, America's great bridges, the interstate highway system, and the space program. Likewise, the abolitionist movement, women's suffrage, the labor movement, and civil rights were all progressive movements. The Fourteenth Amendment, which guarantees equal protection under the law, much like all the other amendments, was a progressive initiative. Some of these projects we may look back on as successful and good programs, and others we may later view as disasters. Either way, such projects come from a commitment to American progress and are paid for from the pubic treasury for the benefit of society. Because of its basis in hope, progressivism provides the lens that shows where the system is unfair, preferential, or exclusive.

Legitimate progressivism originates in the inspired energy of hope, and is the source of our renowned American optimism even as it perceives most clearly our deepest problems. It is legitimate because it is an integrated, connected energy that serves the needs of society to move forward and address its challenges. Progressive sensibilities acknowledge that sometimes government needs to play an integral role in creating an environment for the public good. Even as far back as the Revolution, quasi-governmental organizations were established to meet these needs, and resulted in early projects like the Erie Canal. Basic utilities like water, sewer, electricity, and rural electrification were also provided under progressive programs. Progressivism leads the culture in understanding the necessity of infrastructure for the freeing of the human spirit. Inspired by hope, it converts directly into real, on-the-ground projects that help people.

While trying to create an environment in which freedom, prosperity, and inspiration can flourish, progressive energy can also go too far. When progressive sensibility spills over from guaranteed infrastructure—like building good roads—to an effort to guarantee *outcomes*—such as telling people where they may gather and with whom they may meet—progressivism leans away from liberal principle. In the hands of rigid thinkers and ideologues, *illegitimate* progressivism asserts the control necessary to achieve those guaranteed outcomes. Such control leads progressivism toward dictatorial socialism or communism.[14]

Progressive ideas become dissociated and illegitimate when they disconnect from their foundation on liberal principles. For example, as they move to the left, progressives tend to de-emphasize the importance of profit in the American liberal economic system. Profits are the fruits of creative economic enterprise, yet progressives sometimes see profit as an obscenity that unfairly exploits the fruits of labor. Exploitation of workers, especially when corporate structures are so endemic to our economic way of life, can be common, and such exploitation is anathema to liberty. Profit, on the other hand, is necessary. Liberal economics requires that people are free to deploy capital and labor according to their own judgment, and to

---

[14] Hayek, Freidrich. *The Road to Serfdom*. University of Chicago Press, Chicago, 1944. Hayek's warning to the West centered on the idea that a sympathy for socialism can become nationalized fascism because of the control necessarily exerted to achieve the socialist goals. He saw socialism play a significant role in national movements in Germany, Italy, Spain, Greece, and Russia as each brought nationalistic dictators to power with the help of socialists.

enjoy the fruits of those decisions. The confusion of exploitation with profit is a misunderstanding of the liberal economic principle. When they make this mistake, progressive positions become extreme and illegitimate. Liberalism demands a discerning balance.

As another example, in the 1990s Bill McKibben, the acclaimed environmental writer, seriously proposed a "solution" for the great plains—tear down all the fences from North Dakota to Oklahoma, remove the farms and ranches, and bring back the buffalo to roam free as they once did. The progressive hope and willingness to change fueled this idea as a way to stop soil erosion, recover biodiversity, and engage environmental restoration. On the other hand, it would create forced resettlement and the taking of private land, both of which violate liberal principle of individual sovereignty and private property, respectively. How do you take the land? How do you move the people? Who says we should destroy those communities instead of others? This was progressivism unhinged. Dissociated and ungrounded on principle, it was completely illegitimate in a modern liberal society.

The old communist scare died with the Soviet Union in 1989, but many Americans remain nervous when they contend with progressive ideas that look collectivist. The fear is also raised when progressive ideas manifest as currents of American culture: for example, anti-poverty programs become entitlements, political and social awareness become a code of political correctness and thought-policing, and racial diversity becomes racial and ethnic quotas. These illegitimate collapses are the Achilles Heel of progressivism: they are where progressive ideas dissociate from the principles, seek to control outcomes for others, and think themselves better able to determine good behavior than people can for themselves. Here, the progressive impulse denies individual sovereignty and seeks to restore itself as the "priestly" class standing between people and their reality, determining for other people what is best for them, and restoring pre-modern consciousness and its culture of honor, order, duty, and allegiance.

Legitimate progressivism avoids these problems. It does not dissociate from the principles, so it remains a critical part of the liberal debate. When legitimate progressivism champions change, fairness and fact, it stands up for increased freedom and opportunity for everyone. And, of course, it holds up progressive hope. Nonetheless, the legitimate progressive style will find itself in debate with the legitimate moderate and conservative styles, and such debate is useful and important so long as the three styles do not dissociate from the liberal principle. Our debates and political discussions suffer when we dissociate from our own legitimate position, or when any opposition is automatically assumed to be dissociated, and therefore illegitimate. Those are the conditions that shut down conversation.

Now that we have seen how this works in the progressive modality, let's turn to the moderate.

The Moderate Modality

Moderate political energy lies at the heart of a well-functioning democracy, and, most of the time, at the heart of a livable society. The legitimate energies of moderation include compromise, gradualism, tolerance, consensus, stability, and—somewhat paradoxically—self-interest. Moderate sensibility is about coming into accordance with one's neighbors. It seeks to develop solutions to problems that are acceptable to the majority and is therefore essential to the legislative and governing process of liberal democracy. Moderates understand that their own interest will be well-served by communal acts and decisions that serve everyone—a better community for all means a better community for each individual. And moderates are willing to work slowly and diligently to achieve the improved community, maintain stability, and achieve gradual change that is needed in modern society.

Liberal democratic institutions require compromise and consensus in order to function, and they also require appropriate representation of self interest. The idea of negotiating "in good faith" highlights the need for honest, self-interested negotiation. As such, the moderate modality stands firmly on the principle of individual sovereignty.

Genuine self-interest is essential to compromise, gradualism, and tolerance; all of which require a robust sense of self-interest in order to function. This self-interest, however, must be understood in relationship to the larger community—be that a family, neighborhood, state, or nation. Genuine self-interest requires knowing oneself enough to recognize the power of an improved community in supporting and improving one's own life. In other words, self-interest promotes interest in finding solutions in the communities, families, and nations in which we live. Without self-interest, there is no basis for negotiation, no basis for compromise, no basis for the hard work of developing solutions and implementing them over time.

Real moderation sounds sleepy, but requires us to stay awake because there are two ways for moderate sensibility to dissociate and become illegitimate. First, moderates must be alert to who they are engaged with, and whether or not the partner in compromise possesses real substance, argues from a legitimate place, and negotiates in good faith. Does the other party espouse ideas that are legitimate and tolerable? How does one compromise with a bully? An avowed racist? A Nazi? It can be like negotiating with a drunk. The illegitimate moderate falls asleep and fails to take heed of his or her negotiating opponent. He recalls his favorite words: compromise, tolerate, go slow. But his lack of vigilance leads him to compromise with tyranny, to tolerate the intolerable, and therefore to use moderation to betray the very values and principles at the core of this style of democracy. The moderate modality fails when the moderate person abdicates his responsibility to properly assess the opponent before entering negotiation.

Moderate sensibility also dissociates into isolationism. Dissociated moderates look at the world and say: "Well, I'm okay, so the world must be okay." This perspective betrays what Ken Wilber has identified as narcissism at the center of our culture—"it all revolves around me."[15] My home, my job, my secure island that keeps the rest of the world away and my world neat and tidy. "My life is okay, I'm being protected from terrorists, my taxes are low. Guess I will vote the status quo." Here, the moderate

---

[15] Wilber, Ken. *Boomeritis*. Shambala, Boston, 2002.

view to maintaining a good world dissociates into a selfish focus on one's own situation, exclusive to the community.

For the moderate approach, one compromises and develops a reasoned dialogue. Moderates have strength here, but they too often fall under the spell of the liberal-conservative split and believe that their right-wing or left-wing extreme opponents really share the moderate's desire to improve the world, govern well, and create fair and just outcomes for more people. True conservatives support these goals, as do progressives, but the extreme positions want nothing of the sort. Genuine moderates do not bankrupt the government, tolerate incompetence or send us to needless war.

Vigilance is required in order to ensure that moderate instincts do not collapse into a lack of consciousness or awareness of the challenges and opportunities that surround us. Millions of Americans have fallen under the spell of this form of illegitimate moderatism—most of them good, caring people. But in lowering their vigilance, many take for granted things that generations before us fought for, protected, studied, and earned.

The Conservative Modality

The conservative modality is the third key aspect of a healthy liberal body politic. Legitimate conservatism anchors the cultural base and keeps the progressives from flying too high and too far. Real conservatives constantly ask the questions: *What will we value from our past? As we move into the future, what do we not want to discard?*

How do we conserve the good that we have achieved? Are we really thinking well here? Do we know the limits?

Conservatism conserves. It conserves the past, our traditions, our good ideas. It conserves wealth, profit, and free enterprise. It conserves our achievements and resources. The environmental movement is essentially conservative, even though it is considered a progressive issue today. Conservatism believes that government should be sufficient, but small. Real conservatism is suspicious of government intervention in our lives, tends to support and defend civil liberties, favors fiscal responsibility, and, more often than not, tends toward isolationism rather than interventionism and imperialism. Conservative thought insists on a real reckoning with limits, and insists on rigorous thought and an honest confrontation with pragmatic reality.

Legitimate conservatism doesn't dissociate from its liberal principles. For example, conservatism defends the sovereignty of every individual. It abhors the invasion of privacy covered under the fourth amendment by unreasonable search and seizure every bit as much as the attempt to legislate the private reproductive lives of men and women. The true conservative sees both for what they are – unwarranted encroachments of individual sovereignty. Hence, they reject these positions.

Likewise, the legitimate conservative position on Rule of Law focuses on legal traditions, the importance of precedent, and other aspects of the law. For example, the framers were aligned with conservatism when they built our legal system on the foundation of English common law. They kept much of value from that slowly developed, widely held set of legal principles. Even though much in that law and that system was the cause of the Revolution.

My point is that conservatism is not an alternative to liberalism; rather it is a mode of liberalism that both serves it and is served by it. They go together, depend on one another, and exist in mutual synergy. That is not to say conservatism can't go wrong; it can.

Like the moderate modality, conservatism dissociates in two common ways. First, it dissociates through its "traditional values" rhetoric, which is really code for an anti-modern, anti-progress ideology. It manifests as a "turning the clock back" on truly liberal and liberalizing progress. The words "traditional values" don't mean preserving what's good in this context. Rather, when used as cover or code, really mean: "Put the women back in their place; put the father back in charge; move the minorities out of the neighborhood, the schools, and the jobs." In other words, traditional values is a cover term for perceived pre-modern advantages that people want to recover for themselves—advantages that are to be regained by removing the sovereignty of other individuals, taking their property, and changing their Rule of Law. Such views push the country backward. Legitimate conservatives do not seek to go backward.

The other primary conservative dissociation disguises itself as a pro-business mentality. The effect of most so-called pro-business policies, however, is the concentration of power, profit, and money in the hands of a few, usually through the structure of corporations. This illegitimacy has arisen periodically in American history: Think of the robber-barons and how they developed markets, monopolies, oligopolies, and cartels to effectively control the American economy and build their wealth by eliminating opportunity for others. The rhetoric may sound pro-business, but it is actually oriented toward retention of their own power, wealth, and position. This position leans toward a hybrid of aristocracy and fascism, rather than a real conservative discipline of fiscal responsibility.

Perhaps the worst of the conservative energy can be seen in the forces that fought against our country's most important reform movements, starting with the Revolution. What were the Tories if not conservative? Too often, illegitimate conservatism has found itself on the wrong side of critical issues: abolition of slavery, empowering working people, uniform voting rights for women and African Americans, the civil rights movement. In these cases, "conservatives" fought for the morally reprehensible on the basis that the practices in question have become a traditional part of the fabric of society. They did so not out of conservative fealty to liberal principle, but from a dissociated position. Such positions can never be accepted as legitimate in liberal society, for the more accepted they become, the more our liberty wanes.

Legitimate conservative concern recognizes the good in what we have created in America, and seeks to maintain it. We are blessed by the genius of our Constitution and the people who created it. We are also blessed by a strong heritage of Enlightenment principles, rational thought, religious inspiration, and entrepreneurial creativity. We have a rich natural world in which to act, and many of our best traditions go back hundreds of years. Real conservatism seeks to conserve these traditions and resources and to maintain our wealth and our independence, both individually and as a nation. Conservatism is wary of change because of the danger inherent in losing what is good from our past. These impulses are critical for maintaining stability in the political, economic and religious spheres in which we operate, and where our real, liberated spirit can be free.

Reclaiming the Words

When they are legitimate, progressives, moderates, and conservatives all proceed from a *liberal* worldview. Each standpoint sees certain issues clearly, while other problems go unheeded. Each standpoint possesses certain tools it uses regularly, while others remain unused. And yet, all three standpoints hold to the principles of American liberalism. We are not dealing with a "liberal-conservative split," but rather a split between principled American liberalism—which includes progressive, moderate, and conservative—and extreme ideologies which lie outside the tradition of American liberal democracy.

Right-wing ideologies are a good example. America as a Christian theocracy is not an American principle. Making war for purposes other than self-defense is not an American principle. Making a law to affect one person is not an American principle. Spying on Americans without warrant betrays a disdain of American principle, and the preference for church-based organizations violates the most basic American and modern principle of church-state separation. Right-wing, non-conservative forces promoted all of these examples recently. Left-wing ideological positions supporting communism are equally as egregious. Legitimate progressives, moderates and conservatives all find these ideologies on both sides reprehensible—not because they oppose their own values, but because they oppose the very foundation of liberal society. Legitimate conservatives oppose right-wing extremists just as legitimate progressives oppose communist extremists—in both cases they do so because they realize that the enemy is not their worthy opponent in a legitimate debate, but rather the person whose position would undermine and destroy the very right to such a debate if it were to prevail. That is, they see the enemy in the extreme position as the clear, and obviously non-liberal thing that it really is.

In each given age, the nation is challenged to deal with loud extreme voices from one side or the other. At this time in America, the ascending voice emanates from the extreme right wing, and to understand its impact on the body politic, we need to listen to those who know it the best. That is the task to which we turn now.

CHAPTER FOUR

True Conservatives Disenfranchised

The extreme positions of the right wing are often criticized by progressives and moderates, but such critiques are usually viewed as ideological or self-serving, and therefore easily and frequently dismissed. However, the evidence that the right-wing is not conservative comes from the legitimate conservatives themselves, who can see clearly that non-conservative, extreme ideas have hijacked the word *conservative*. Many are deeply concerned, and occasionally they publish their thoughts. In Ron Suskind's book, *The Price of Loyalty*, Former Treasury Secretary Paul O'Neill portrays a real understanding of finances from a conservative perspective:

> ...the budget is often the only place where there is a true competition of disparate ideas—a competition over who will get the money and who won't. And the only way for that competition to work is for the budget to be finite. A ballooning deficit... is a sign of casual thinking and tough choices not being made. Balancing a budget, thereby, is not just a matter of fiscal good sense. It compels companion virtues—such as intellectual rigor and honest assessment of

the intentions that underlie action. Do you know what you're doing—and do you know why?[16]

O'Neill's view here is decidedly conservative in its high regard for limits, demand for rigorous thought, embrace of competition as a principle, and requirement of a certain kind of discipline. Yet O'Neill's statement is also profoundly liberal for all the same reasons.

The Price of Loyalty also tells the now infamous story of a 2001 oval office discussion over deficits, the impact of high deficits and accelerating debt, and the possible fiscal crisis portended by the economic policies of the 2000-2008 Bush administration. O'Neill argued vehemently for restraint and fiscal discipline. Cheney responded: "Reagan proved deficits don't matter." Initially shocked that his old friend Cheney would say such a thing, O'Neill considered the matter this way:

> I thought that, clearly, there's no coherent philosophy that could support such a claim.... I think an ideology comes out of feelings and tends to be non-thinking. A philosophy, on the other hand, can have a structured thought base. One would hope that a philosophy, which is always a work in progress, is influenced by facts. So there is a constant interplay between *what do I think* and *why do I think it*....
>
> Now, if you gather more facts and have more experience, especially with things that have gone wrong—those are especially good learning tools—then you reshape your philosophy, because the facts tell you you've got to....
>
> Ideology is a lot easier, because you don't have to know anything or search for anything. You already know the

---

[16] Suskind, Ron. *The Price of Loyalty*. Simon & Schuster, New York, 2004, p. 280

answer to everything. It's not penetrable by facts. It's absolutism.[17]

O'Neill reflects his adherence to liberal principles such as reason, the importance of facts, experience as a teacher, and fiscal responsibility. These stand in contrast to radical right-wing ideology which may try to claim them as its own, even though its principles are based on the literal truth of the Bible, free use of power and authority, and non-thinking. O'Neill, a conservative Republican, provides a shining example of how true conservative philosophy is completely consistent with true liberal principle, and how true conservative thought is completely inconsistent with the right-wing ideology, which today controls much of American government.

A second example of a disenfranchised conservative is Christine Todd Whitman, the former rising star of the Republican Party who fell out of grace as she fell out with the Bush administration, left office, and later published her book, *It's My Party, Too*. Whitman's perspective is that the "social fundamentalists" have taken over the party. She is clear about who they are: extreme Christian fundamentalists. "These groups [are] headed by people I call social fundamentalists, whose sole mission is to advance their narrow ideological agenda."[18] But such agendas, she says, are not the core values of conservatism and the Republican Party—values like smaller government, fiscal responsibility, and strong security. Whitman is very specific about how those values should guide policy positions:

---

[17] *Ibid.*, p. 292.
[18] Whitman, Christine Todd. *It's My Party, Too*. Penguin Press, New York, 2005, p 3.

If we believe the government has a responsibility to be prudent in its use of taxpayer dollars and not run up huge deficits that will ultimately tax our children and grandchildren, we must push for fiscal responsibility and should seek to couple tax cuts with restraint on spending.

If we believe that every woman has the right to make choices about her pregnancy, without interference from the government, we must not support appointment of judges who vow to overturn Roe v. Wade.

If we believe that the Constitution protects individual freedom from an intrusive central government, then we must oppose a constitutional amendment to regulate or define marriage, and leave that matter where it belongs—with the states.

If we believe that protecting the environment is essential and is a public responsibility and a Republican issue, we must insist on advancing a pro-active agenda that actually results in cleaner air, purer water, and better protected land.

If we believe the United States has a vital role to play as the world's only superpower in leading the world both with strength and wisdom, then we must push for a foreign policy premised on the understanding that the rest of the world matters to us. We must advocate against becoming ensnared in nation-building enterprises and push for policies that engage us with the world community and show, in the words of the Declaration of Independence, "a decent respect to the opinions of mankind."[19]

The supposition in each of these statements constitutes the core creed of conservatism, but the so-called conservative administration is going in the opposite direction on each of them. As head of the Environmental

---

[19] *Ibid.* p. 12.

Protection Agency, Whitman's opposition on these and other issues led to her parting of the ways with the Bush administration.

Most of Whitman's "conservative" positions are based on liberal principles. She writes of people who once "proudly called themselves liberal Republicans" to illustrate the former reach of the party. And then she asks:

So how, in recent years, has the party allowed itself to become captive of a collection of far-right forces, whose pursuit of their own narrow agendas makes it difficult to govern and even harder to appeal to the great moderate center of the American electorate?[20]

In other words, both her Republican Party and the conservative values she holds dear have been lost, hijacked by the extreme right-wing of the party. Millions of Republicans like herself elected and re-elected George W. Bush, but she laments their simultaneous disenfranchisement from the party. Whitman fears that the extreme right will take over the entire party if something doesn't change. "Preventing that troubling fate will take the emergence of 'radical moderates,'" she claims. Whitman's focus is on her Republican Party; the same risks and the same remedies may apply to America as a whole.

For a third example of disenfranchised conservatives, take Dave Durenberger. The former Minnesota Senator served during the Reagan era and is a true conservative—what I will call a liberal conservative, in that his liberal *principles* outweigh any right-wing *ideology*. He makes his views clear in a March 2005 interview with the Twin Cities weekly *City Pages:*

---

[20] *Ibid.* p. 31.

Today, though—I'll cite Grover Norquist, who said something to the effect of, 'Bipartisanship is like date rape.' And that's what drives people now in the [Republican] party. They talk about freedom and values, but they really don't believe in representative government. They don't see that the country ought not to be divided in half. You're just looking at gridlock.[21]

Durenberger again:

We use the words 'national security' to justify absolutely everything that goes on in this country. And that's not American.

Imagine. A conservative Republican saying that using the words "national security" to justify everything is "not American." But Durenberger is a legitimate conservative, not one of those using the word "conservative" to obscure some hidden agenda. He's not trying to hide a theocratic impulse, a tendency toward fascism, or a right-wing leaning. Durenberger's genuine conservative philosophy is at the heart of his perspective. Like so many conservatives, he is unhappy with how the conservative perspective has been stolen.

Here's part of Durenberger's response about religion in politics:

Do they all come from their own churches and such? Yes. But look. I have very strong feelings about faith as a motivator. You can have your faith, and you can't just check it at the door when you go to work, but there's got to be enough respect to keep it out of what you do. When you start to rely on The Book to set policy, I begin to have a problem

---

[21] G.R Anderson, Jr., *City Pages,* March 9, 2005. Cover Story interview with Dave Durenberger.

with that. I can't handle that one, the business of legislating your faith.... It can't last. It's not foundational as far as America is concerned; it's not foundational as far as representative democracy is concerned. You can bring your faith to your life and your work, but that should also include respect for other people and respect for other opinions.[22]

Many readers will have heard similar ideas from their "liberal" friends. But from a conservative Republican? Durenberger reminds us that "conservative" goes together with liberal principles. In our democracy, the two cannot be separated.

These three examples of genuine conservative philosophy illustrate the difference between real conservatism with its allegiance to the traditions of American liberal principle, and the false right-wing "conservatism" that presently dominates Republican Party politics and the American government. O'Neill, Whitman, and Durenberger all believe in the worldview of American liberal democracy, as do most legitimate conservatives. Most Americans identify such values with the word "conservative," which is precisely why the right-wing co-opted the name "conservative" for themselves.

---

[22] *Ibid.*

CHAPTER FIVE

American Liberal Principles

America was founded during the Enlightenment, a point in history when liberal principles and ideas reached an apex of development. To the framers, liberal principles were the antithesis of tyranny. Some opponents of the Enlightenment, such as Edmund Burke, are celebrated champions of what is now called "conservative". Jonathan Israel described them as leaders of the counter-Enlightenment.[23] The truth is that they were reactionaries attempting to prevent the institution of liberal principles, especially individual sovereignty and they were the first to set up the liberal-conservative split. They opposed the liberal *principles* on which the American Revolution was founded.

In the view of the framers, the alternative to liberal principles and world view was not conservatism; it was tyranny. Again and again, our founding documents refer to these principles and seek to defend them. They don't always use the exact language we'd use today, but all the foundations are there. As we will now see, America is inescapably and unapologetically a modern liberal state.

---

[23] Israel, Jonathan. *Democratic Enlightenment,* Oxford University Press.

Based on Enlightenment ideas, liberal principles, and their own contemporary experiences, American revolutionaries formulated the most famous statements of American liberal principle—the Declaration of Independence, which separated America from tyranny; the Constitution, which created governmental powers to provide checks and balances all modalities of liberal principles; and the Bill of Rights, which specifically enumerated many of the rights the people of the states wished to have protected. Much of the content of these founding documents was previously formulated, developed by colonial legislatures in constitutions, or otherwise emerged in the colonies before independence. Yet, these three documents bring together the unique expression of liberal principles in America, and to the thinking reader they make it clear that America aspires to be a liberal nation, even if she has frequently fallen short.

Declaration of Independence

> We hold these truths to be self-evident, that all men are created equal, that they are endowed by their Creator with certain unalienable rights, that among these are Life, Liberty, and the pursuit of Happiness. That to secure these rights, Governments are instituted among Men, deriving their just powers from the consent of the governed. That whenever any Form of Government becomes destructive of these ends, it is the Right of the People to alter or abolish it, and to institute new Government, laying its foundation on such principles and organizing its powers in such form, as to them shall seem most likely to effect their Safety and Happiness.

This eloquent passage has inspired liberal revolutionaries for centuries. It declared the unalienable rights of man, which are now understood to include every person. What few people understand is its intimate connection to individual sovereignty. The principle of individual sovereignty is the idea of unalienable rights—they are essentially the same thing. As a human being, each individual has the right to personal sovereignty, to not be violated in particular ways, and to live fully and completely in Life, Liberty and the pursuit of Happiness.

Powerful as this idea is, there is a lot more to individual sovereignty. For example, the Declaration says that any government failing in that duty can be altered or abolished, and replaced by a government "deriving their just powers from the consent of the governed." It refers to the "Right of the People to abolish it" and states that the new government may be based "on such principles and organizing its powers in such form, as to them shall seem most likely to effect their Safety and Happiness." All these references to "the people", "the principles", and "them" are references to the liberal principle of individual sovereignty. Indeed, of all the liberal principles, the American revolutionaries perceived none to be as crucial as that one idea. Ultimately, the entire enterprise of America is based on it.

For most Americans, the Declaration of Independence starts and ends with that inspiring paragraph shown above. Few realize that the document goes on for several pages after that. Indeed, the rest of the document lists complaints against the King of Great Britain. A careful reading of the Declaration indicates that the central concern of these complaints was the violation of other liberal principles. In the language of the Revolution, such violations constitute tyranny. To illustrate what I mean, I have extracted sample lines from the text of the Declaration and classified them according to the liberal principle they primarily refer to. Keep in mind that there are many more pages of these complaints against the king, and that these are just a few examples:[24]

> The history of the present King of Great Britain is a history of repeated injuries and usurpations, all having in direct object the establishment of an absolute Tyranny over these States. To prove this, let Facts be submitted to a candid world....

Rule of Law
- *He has refused his Assent to Laws, the most wholesome and necessary for the public good...*
- *He has obstructed the Administration of Justice, by refusing his Assent to Laws for establishing Judiciary powers.*
- He has refused to pass other laws for the accommodation of large districts of people, unless those people would relinquish the right of representation in the legislature, a right inestimable to them and formidable to tyrants only.
- He has made Judges dependent on his Will alone, for the tenure of their offices, and the amount and payment of their salaries.

Private Property
- He has endeavored to prevent the population of these states; for that purpose obstructing the laws for naturalization of foreigners; refusing to pass others to encourage their migration hither, and raising the conditions of new appropriations of lands

---

[24] Ellis, Joseph J. *What Did the Declaration Declare?* Bedford/St. Martin's, Boston-New York, 1999. Excerpts from the Declaration of Independence are taken from this source.

- For quartering large bodies of armed troops among us:
- He has plundered our seas, ravaged our coasts, burned our towns, and destroyed the lives of our people.

Individual Sovereignty
- He has dissolved representative houses repeatedly, for opposing with manly firmness his invasions on the rights of the people.
- He has abdicated government here, by declaring us out of his protection and waging war against us.
- He has kept among us, in time of peace, Standing Armies without the Consent of our legislature.

The litany of complaints against the King constitute a catalog of anti-liberal practices and powers exercised in violation of the liberty of Americans. Although the specific complaints are particular to the time, the offenses are perpetrated against the timeless liberal principles. Liberal principles were the focus of revolutionary America, and there was no such thing as a conservative principle. The only alternative was pre-modern consciousness and the aristocratic, feudal, church-based systems of government and societal organization on which they were based.

The Constitution

The United States of America incorporated liberal philosophy and principle into its its founding documents, structure, and operation. Its opening words "We the People..." invoke the single most unalienable right put forth in the Declaration—the sovereignty of the people and of each individual.

The Constitution, especially in its original form, was hardly a perfect document. It was very strong in protecting the liberty of white, land-owning men, while its treatment of women, slaves, Native Americans, and the landless was abysmal. In this way, it was a nascent, immature document, even though profoundly original, and it was destined to grow and change, just as the framers expected. Yet for all its flaws and shortcomings, it was the first Constitution that formed a government based on liberal principles.

The liberal sensibilities are built into the document and the structure of the government it created. What's famous from that are the three branches, checks and balances on power, elections, the electoral college, and even the process for amending the constitution. These mechanics of government provided the method for ongoing representative democracy and republican government. But what is fascinating and less noticed are the subtle ways the modalities of liberal principles are layered in.

The Constitution is a hierarchy of ideas expressed as the mechanics of government. *Regulations*, promulgated and enforced by the *executive* branch, tend to lead change, and are therefore primarily *progressive* in nature, and deal with things which are easily changed. The *laws* of the land, passed by the *legislature*, reflect the will of the people and are *moderate* in nature. They reflect compromise between competing interests, viewpoints or positions. The liberal *principles* on which the nation is founded are guarded by the *judiciary*. This level of the hierarchy is inherently *conservative*, preserving our commitment to the principles of self-government, liberty, and freedom. Finally, the most conservative aspect of all, the *philosophical* roots of the nation, are expressed in the *Constitution*. This level expresses the *dogma* of liberal government and society, and requires the assent of Congress, the President, and three fourths of the state legislatures for amendment. Taken together, these constitute the political expression of the American form of liberal consciousness.

The subtleties of these layers are often missed in the focus on checks and balances, but it is rarely asked who is checking what. The checks and balances are between the three modalities—progressive, moderate, and conservative—and their purpose is to prevent any modality from dissociating its politics and bringing down the entire edifice. The moderate legislature checks a progressive executive, a progressive executive challenges conservative judiciary, and so on.

The insidious problem of the liberal-conservative split is herein revealed. The conservative side of this split is actually not conservative of liberal principles at all—it is dissociated conservatism which seeks to turn the entire country into a right wing nation. If the extreme ideas underlying dissociated conservatism are allowed to masquerade as conservative, the check and balance fails. First, the true conservative modality is no longer represented at all. Second, one of the "check and balance" powers is dissociated into a non-liberal perspective that really sees liberal principles as its enemy. In other words, it's like inviting the known, unrepentant, committed criminal into your home. He who invites such a man should not be surprised when he is drugged and wakes up to find all his possessions stolen. As so-called conservatives, who are actually right-wing ideologues, are increasingly accepted as legitimate conservatives, we are in danger of making exactly the same mistake, and we should not be surprised when a similar nightmare begins.

Bill of Rights

The expression of America's liberal philosophy is also found in the Bill of Rights, the critical first ten amendments to the Constitution which helped to broker and seal the deal between the states, wherein the rights of religious, political, and economic minorities, down to a single individual, are protected. Like the Constitution, the Bill of Rights addresses a lot more than just the primary principles of liberal society. Still, it is intriguing to see just how much these roles appear in, and probably drove, the creation of the Bill of Rights. Here are a few examples.

Perhaps the most famous amendment of all is the first amendment, which reads as follows:

> Congress shall make no law respecting an establishment of religion, or prohibiting the free exercise thereof; or abridging the freedom of speech, or of the press; or the right of the people peaceably to assemble, and to petition the government for a redress of grievances.

Separation of church and state , freedom of speech, and freedom of the press are directly addressed to the philosophical differentiation of religion, politics, and economics which we discussed earlier. The right to assemble, speak, and petition all harken to the individual sovereignty principle. Of course there is much more in these words, and entire books have been written on this amendment alone. For our purpose, it is enough to note the the tie to the basic principles as well as the underlying consciousness of modernity.

The fourth amendment is a protection of individual sovereignty, ensuring that we cannot be searched or our property seized without just cause.

> The right of the people to be secure in their persons, houses, papers, and effects, against unreasonable searches and seizures, shall not be violated, and no warrants shall issue, but upon probable cause, supported by oath or affirmation, and particularly describing the place to be searched, and the persons or things to be seized.

If one reads the Bill of Rights next to the Declaration of Independence, it is easy to see that many of the amendments in the Bill of Rights are a direct response to the complaints leveled in the Declaration. This is significant because the two documents are separated by over twelve years. The issues covered in the two documents derive from enduring concerns of the framers.

The Bill of Rights also demonstrates how America started with a relatively limited, nascent application of these rights, and has slowly fulfilled them over the years. The Bill of Rights was originally designed to limit only the powers of the federal government—states could, and often did, establish policies which would later be seen as violations of civil liberties. This interpretation of the Bill of Rights was reinforced in an 1833 case, Barron v. Baltimore, by the Supreme Court. Chief Justice John Marshall, speaking for a unanimous Court, determined that the Bill of Rights applies to actions of the federal government, and not to those of the individual states.

After the Civil War (1865), Congress passed and states ratified the 14th Amendment, whose first section—the so-called "due process and equal protection" clause—ought to have ensured that the rights of blacks in the south were not eliminated or infringed. It guaranteed that the rights and privileges of all citizens could not be abridged by the state governments. Beginning in 1920s, the Supreme Court began to affirm in several decisions that the first section of the 14th amendment did in fact mean the protections in the Bill of Rights applied to local and state governments as well as the federal government. In many ways, these decisions were the strongest statement our country has ever made on individual sovereignty, except perhaps for those opening three words of the Constitution.

Conclusion

This survey of the historical development of liberal principles and liberal society now comes full circle, to today. The rhetoric of the liberal-conservative split continues, and is as damaging as ever to the American body politic. It is my hope that with the new understanding framed in these pages, the reader may consider a reassessment of that rhetoric. At its core, it is a false rhetoric, a false divide. When demonstrable falseness has been injected into a public debate and become the dominant frame of that debate, it can usually be traced to one of two underlying causes—the ignorance of the people or a purposeful distortion, which is otherwise known as propaganda. In this case, as is so often true, it is both. Most Americans are ignorant of this history and its development. Without knowledge of this history, we heard the liberal-conservative split repeated over and over again, and it is only human psychology to eventually accept that which you hear, especially if you hear no coherent, countervailing statements. The lack of such statements is our ignorance shining through. This book hopes to disengage such ignorance from its dominant place in our society.

At the same time, we cannot discount the propaganda, for this idea of a liberal-conservative split serves someone, or the media would not be repeating it. I have made the argument that it serves mostly the extreme right-wing agenda in America, but the notion of such a split can serve any agenda that is essentially opposed to the fundamental principles of a liberal society. The examples of Paul O'Neill, Dave Durenberger, and Christine Todd Whitman were from the early Bush era, and presaged what has been developing since. "Liberals" continue to be demonized, and, more importantly, the ideas and principles of liberal society are going with it. The financiers and activists who would denigrate the very foundation of American society must, in the end, offer a solution—what would they replace it with? One thing should be clear: It would not be liberal principle.

In this way, our collective ignorance serves the propagandists. Because we do not recognize ourselves as a liberal society, because we do not know what liberal principles are and how our entire way of life is based on them, because we can't see ourselves clearly as conservative, moderate, or progressive, yet all and always as liberal, we are collectively susceptible to the deceptive claim of a liberal-conservative split. In reality, the split we should be concerned about is not the liberal-conservative split, but rather the division between all the Americans who fall on the liberal continuum, from legitimate progressive to legitimate conservative, and those extreme few who are truly radical in their vision for a society and government organized on a set of principles that is not liberal at all. History has shown that most such societies are not good places to live. Communism and fascism, socialism and despotism, theocracy and plutocracy, dictatorship and totalitarianism are all alternatives we have witnessed. Who among us would choose these over liberal democratic society?

Those who demonize liberal principles in America share common interest with those who demonize liberal principles from outside our great nation. The strongest global voices against liberal principles today in that regard are Islamic fundamentalists—ISIS, the Taliban, al Qaeda,

Boko Harem. Yet we also have Vladimir Putin, the various former Soviet states of south central Asia, and many other examples. Their critiques and hatreds of "liberals" are as sharp and as clear as those of our own home-grown right-wing extremists. We can all see, for example, the awful threat of ISIS and its ideology, and they are open not only about what they hate—liberal ideas and principles—but also about what they want—a fundamentalist caliphate under a theocratic rule of terror. On the other hand, the opponents of liberal principle in America have yet to say what they would replace these principles with. They have argued we are a Christian nation, thus pointing toward theocracy, but not claiming it. They have acted to reinforce corporate power, thus hinting toward plutocracy. When in power, they have initiated ideas such as unitary executive, thus suggesting interest in dictatorial power. Yet none have fully articulated the vision in full site for Americans to see. Of course, there is a reason for this—if they did, we would soundly reject it.

...at least, I would hope so. The risk is that we might not reject it because of our ignorance, and as I said earlier, my hope in writing this book is to thwart such ignorance. We Americans are some of the most privileged people in the world. For all our problems as a country, there remain billions of people who would trade places with any one of us if given a choice. People are still trying to get into this country, not trying to escape it. We are extremely fortunate, and even as we fight the international battles to hold back anti-liberal ideologies, let us also watch carefully for the anti-liberal ideologies developing among us. Those ideologies, which are *out there*, and the ignorance, which is *within each individual*, can become a lethal team in the defeat of our own liberty and the usurpation of our shared liberal principles. Fortunately, one of our very strongest weapons, *intelligence*, is completely within us and under our own control. Let's use it to defend the great principles that have been given to us, and the great privilege we have to live in a country founded upon them.

About the Author

Anthony Signorelli is the author of several books on postcapitalism and political philosophy. He also blogs and publishes Intertwine, a regular email for deep hearts and vital minds.

To join the conversation and find out more about these books and Intertwine, please visit

http://anthonysignorelli.com/books

Made in the USA
Middletown, DE
28 September 2018